FROM SEA to SHINING SEA

WEST VIRGINIA

BARBARA A. SOMERVILL

Consultants

MELISSA N. MATUSEVICH, PH.D.

Curriculum and Instruction Specialist
Blacksburg, Virginia

SUZETTE LOWE

Director, Roane County Library
Spencer, West Virginia

GEORGINA DOSS

Manager
Milton Branch Cabell Public Libraries
Milton, West Virginia

CHILDREN'S PRESS®

A DIVISION OF SCHOLASTIC INC.

New York • Toronto • London • Auckland • Sydney • Mexico City
New Delhi • Hong Kong • Danbury, Connecticut

West Virginia is in the southeastern part of the United States. It is bordered by Virginia, Maryland, Pennsylvania, Ohio, and Kentucky.

The photograph on the front cover shows Harpers Ferry and Harpers Ferry National Historical Park.

Project Editor: Meredith DeSousa
Art Director: Marie O'Neill
Photo Researcher: Marybeth Kavanagh
Design: Robin West, Ox and Company, Inc.
Page 6 map and recipe art: Susan Hunt Yule
All other maps: XNR Productions, Inc.

Library of Congress Cataloging-in-Publication Data

Somervill, Barbara A.
    West Virginia / Barbara A. Somervill.
      p. cm. -- (From sea to shining sea)
Summary: Takes the reader on a tour of the Mountain State, emphasizing its geography, history, government, and culture.
Includes bibliographical references (p.   ) and index.
    0-516-22389-5
    1. West Virginia--Juvenile literature. [1. West Virginia.] I. Title. II. Series.
    F241.3 .S66 2003
    975.4—dc21   2002009109

TABLE of CONTENTS

INTRODUCING THE MOUNTAIN STATE

West Virginia offers some of the best whitewater rafting in the East. This group enjoys a wild ride on the Gauley River.

W**hen you think of West Virginia,** what comes to mind? You might dream about whitewater rafting. More than 200,000 people enjoy rafting on West Virginia's fast-flowing rivers each year. These rushing waterways run through rocky valleys and beautiful forests. You might also picture earth mounds built more than three thousand years ago by West Virginia's earliest people. To learn about the state's rich past, and its present, let's take a journey together into the wild, rugged mountains of West Virginia.

West Virginia is called the Mountain State because mountains cover four in every five acres (1.6 in every 2 hectares) of its land. The peaks and valleys throughout West Virginia draw hunters in the fall, skiers during winter, and hikers throughout the year. Even the state motto, *Montani semper liberi,* is about mountains. It is Latin for "Mountaineers are always free." When West Virginia broke away from Virginia and became a separate state, its people chose a motto that explained their feelings.

The state motto is printed on the state seal, which offers more clues about West Virginia. The center of the seal has a stone with the date West Virginia became a state. You'll also find a farmer and a miner pictured on the seal. In the past, West Virginia's economy was based on farming and mining.

What else comes to mind when you think of West Virginia?

- Moundsville, the site of North America's largest cone-shaped prehistoric earthworks
- Artists creating beautiful works of stained glass
- Whitewater rafting on the Gauley River
- Brother fighting brother during the Civil War
- Students taking classes at West Virginia University
- Railroad cars overflowing with coal
- Daniel Boone blazing a trail through the Appalachian Mountains
- Lost World Caverns, the site of fabulous natural wonders

West Virginia is tree-covered mountains and fast-running rivers. It is apple orchards, coal mines, and ski resorts. As you read this book, you will learn about wild and wonderful West Virginia, the Mountain State.

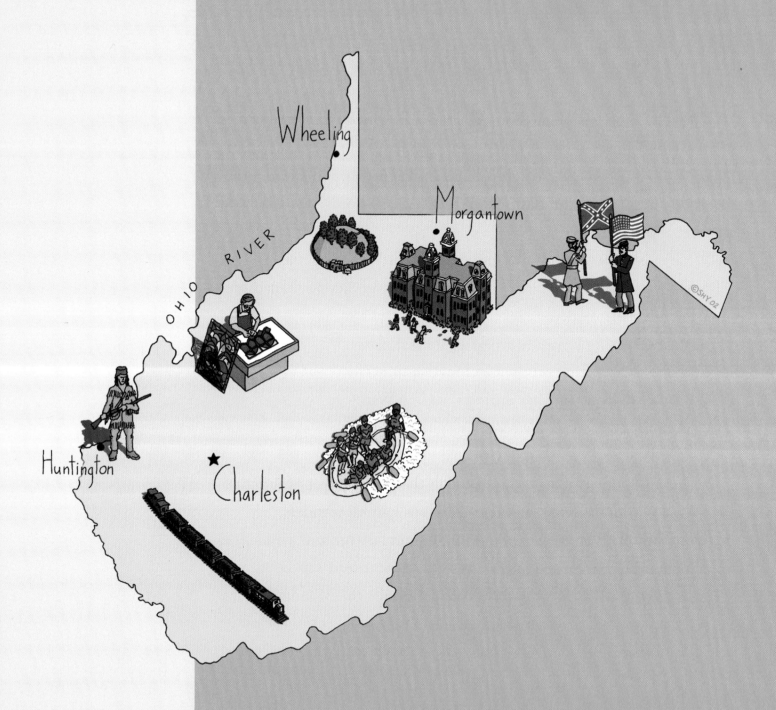

Wheeling

OHIO RIVER

Morgantown

Huntington

Charleston

©SHY 02

CHAPTER TWO

THE LAND OF WEST VIRGINIA

Although it was originally part of the Virginia colony, West Virginia remained unexplored for many years. The Allegheny Mountains were difficult to cross and the land was alive with black bears, white-tailed deer, bobcats, and wild turkeys. The region challenged settlers with tree-covered mountains and fast-rushing streams. Compared to the flat coastal plain of the east, West Virginia was rugged and wild.

Today, rivers and mountains set many of West Virginia's boundaries. The Ohio and Big Sandy rivers flow along the western border with Ohio and Kentucky. The Potomac River marks the northeastern border with Maryland. The Allegheny Mountains mark the border with Virginia. Only the northern border with Pennsylvania has no natural boundary.

The Mountain State is small in area. Forty other states are larger than West Virginia, which occupies 24,231 square miles (62,758 square kilo-

The Monongahela National Forest covers more than 900,000 acres (364,217 ha) in eastern West Virginia.

FIND OUT MORE

A panhandle is a narrow section of land that juts out from the main land area. Look at a map of the United States. What other states have panhandles?

meters). The state has an odd shape—much like a frying pan with two handles. One handle reaches north between Pennsylvania and Ohio. The other stretches to the east. These regions are called panhandles.

LAND REGIONS OF WEST VIRGINIA

West Virginia has two main land regions: the Appalachian Ridge and Valley and the Appalachian Plateau. Both regions lie within the Appalachian Mountain Range. This range runs from Georgia to Maine.

The Appalachian Ridge and Valley Region

The Appalachian Ridge and Valley covers a wide strip of land along the state's eastern border. The Ridge and Valley region also includes most of the eastern panhandle. The Allegheny mountain range in the Appalachian Mountains forms most of this region.

Many mountains between 2,500 and 4,000 feet (762 and 1,219 meters) dot the Ridge and Valley region. These include Keeney Mountain, Bickett Knob, Bald Knob, and Cheat Mountain. You'll also find Spruce Knob in the Ridge and Valley region. It is the highest point in the state at 4,861 feet (1,482 m) above sea level.

Coal mines are common in this area. Stone, sand, and gravel are also quarried there. You'll find plenty of hog, poultry, and sheep farms nestled

A mountain climber scales Seneca Rocks, one of the best known landmarks in eastern West Virginia.

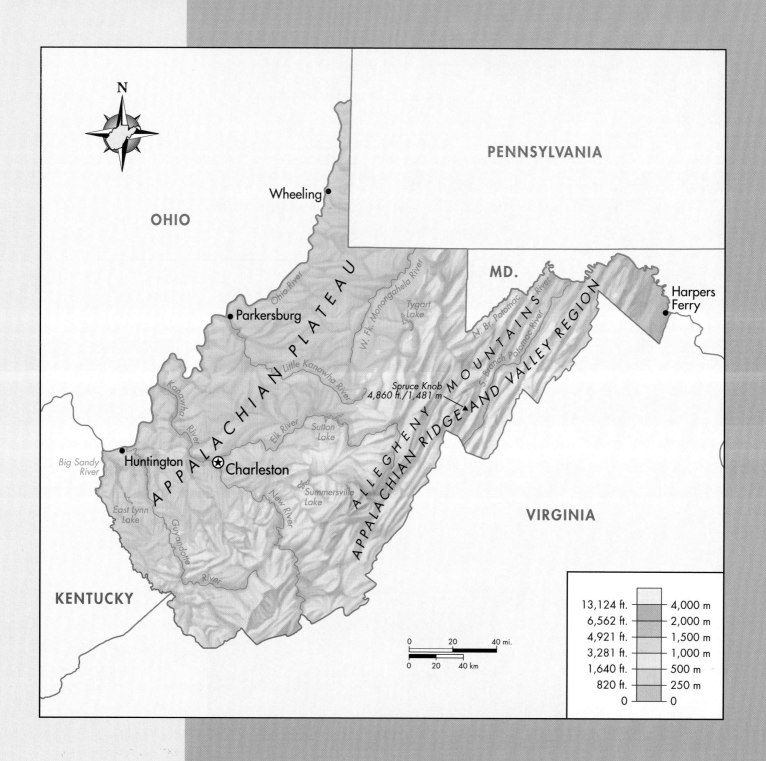

N

PENNSYLVANIA

OHIO

Wheeling

MD.

Harpers
Ferry

Ohio River

Parkersburg

APPALACHIAN PLATEAU

W. Fk. Monongahela River

Tygart
Lake

N. Br. Potomac River

S. Branch Potomac River

Little Kanawha River

ALLEGHENY MOUNTAINS

APPALACHIAN RIDGE AND VALLEY REGION

Spruce Knob
4,860 ft./1,481 m

Kanawha River

Elk River

Sutton
Lake

Big Sandy
River

Huntington

⊛ Charleston

Summersville
Lake

*East Lynn
Lake*

New River

VIRGINIA

Guyandotte

River

KENTUCKY

0   20   40 mi.

0   20   40 km

13,124 ft.	4,000 m
6,562 ft.	2,000 m
4,921 ft.	1,500 m
3,281 ft.	1,000 m
1,640 ft.	500 m
820 ft.	250 m
0	0

in the region's many valleys. Fruit orchards are found on the eastern panhandle. The most common fruits grown there are apples and peaches.

The Appalachian Plateau

The Appalachian Plateau lies between the Ohio River Valley and the Appalachian Ridge and Valley region. It covers about two-thirds of the state from the edge of the Appalachian Ridge to the western border.

The plateau features steep gorges, irregular hills, and broad valleys. Farming is the main source of income in this region. Common crops in this area include corn, tobacco, oats, hay, and grapes. There are also beef cattle ranches, and poultry and dairy farms.

Most of the state's largest cities lie within the Appalachian Plateau. Wheeling, Parkersburg, and Huntington were built along the Ohio River. Charleston, the state's largest city, lies in the center of the region.

RIVERS AND LAKES

The state's largest river is the Ohio River in the west. The Ohio River stretches far beyond West Virginia. It begins in Pittsburgh, Pennsylvania, and runs 981 miles (1,579 kilometers) to Cairo, Illinois. There, the Ohio empties into the Mississippi River. Only 270 miles (435 km) of the Ohio River touches West Virginia.

The Ohio provides shipping for West Virginia's businesses. It has been used for barge and flatboat travel since the early 1700s. Today, boating and fishing add to the bustle on the Ohio River.

Dunloup Creek is in West Virginia's scenic New River Gorge region.

Several smaller rivers, called tributaries, feed the Ohio River. These include the Kanawha, the Guyandotte, the Little Kanawha, and the Big Sandy. The New and Elk rivers run into the Kanawha and flow westward through the lower half of West Virginia. Along the eastern panhandle, the Potomac flows toward the Atlantic Ocean. In eastern West Virginia, the Potomac has both a north and a south branch.

EXTRA! EXTRA!

The New River may be the oldest river in North America. How did scientists figure out the age of the New River? They studied the layers of rock that the river cut through. By using fossils and carbon dating, scientists figured out that the New River cut through some of the rock 320 to 330 million years ago. That makes the New River. . . old!

The rugged New River flows north through deep canyons.

Although West Virginia has many swift rivers and streams, there are few naturally formed lakes. Most lakes in the state were made by damming rivers. Engineers build cement dams to control the flow of river water. The dam blocks off part of a valley or gorge, and the basin fills with river water to form a lake, or reservoir.

Man-made lakes in West Virginia include Summersville, Sutton, East Lynn, and Tygart. The only natural lake is Trout Pond in Hardy County. West Virginia lakes provide drinking water and opportunities for fishing and recreational boating.

West Virginia's forests offer much in the way of scenic beauty and recreational opportunities.

Four in every five acres of West Virginia is forest. At lower altitudes, there are hardwoods, such as wild cherry, oak, elm, sugar maple, beech, walnut, and tulip trees. Hardwoods are ideal for making furniture, which is big business in West Virginia. In the fall, West Virginia's hills come alive with brilliant yellows, hot oranges, and deep reds. These hardwoods give way to evergreens higher up in the mountains. Typical evergreens in West Virginia are red spruce, white pine, and hemlock.

Spring in West Virginia explodes with black-eyed Susans. Soft pink rhododendrons bloom beside wild azaleas, lacy dogwood, and white hawthorn. Wild orchids thrive in the damp forests of West Virginia. These blossoms give way to summer daisies, then fall asters and vivid yellow goldenrod, as splotches of color paint West Virginia's meadows and hillsides.

Mammals, birds, and a variety of creepy creatures thrive in the wilds of West Virginia. Among the large mammals is the black bear, the official state animal. Others include white-tailed deer, bobcats, and raccoons. These animals share the woodland with squirrels, groundhogs, opossums, skunks, and minks. Beavers build lodges on the state's many rivers and streams. You'll also find a full array of snakes, toads, frogs, and lizards throughout West Virginia.

Songbirds share West Virginia skies with soaring birds of prey. The cardinal, the official state bird, nests throughout the state, as do wrens, sparrows, bobwhites, and scarlet tanagers. Far above, great horned owls, eagles, and hawks use their magnificent vision to spy rodents and fish hundreds of feet below them. It is a magical sight watching an eagle swoop down and catch a fish in its talons.

There are plenty of fish to catch, as well. The rivers run wild with brook trout, the state fish. Anglers (sports fishers) cast their lines for walleye, bass, carp, and bluegill.

Black bears mainly live in the eastern mountain region of West Virginia.

FIND OUT MORE

Beavers build homes, called *lodges*, from twigs and branches. Choose five other animals and find out the names of their homes.

CLIMATE

West Virginia enjoys a moderate climate. Overall it has cooler temperatures in the mountains than along the rivers or in valleys. Although there are occasional scorching hot days, the average summer temperature is 72°

Blackwater Falls State Park sparkles under a dusting of winter snow.

Fahrenheit (22° Celsius). Summers often bring dramatic storms. Thunder rolls over the mountains, as jagged lightning stretches across cloudy skies.

Winter is cold and damp. Winter temperatures across the state also vary depending on elevation, or height above sea level. The average January temperature is 33° F (.56° C). Winter storms pile on the snow. Annual snowfall ranges from a northerly high of 100 inches (254 cm) to a low of 20 inches (51 cm) in the southern counties.

The average yearly precipitation is 45 inches (114 cm). This includes rainfall, hail, sleet, and melted snow. Precipitation falls in West Virginia about 151 days of the year.

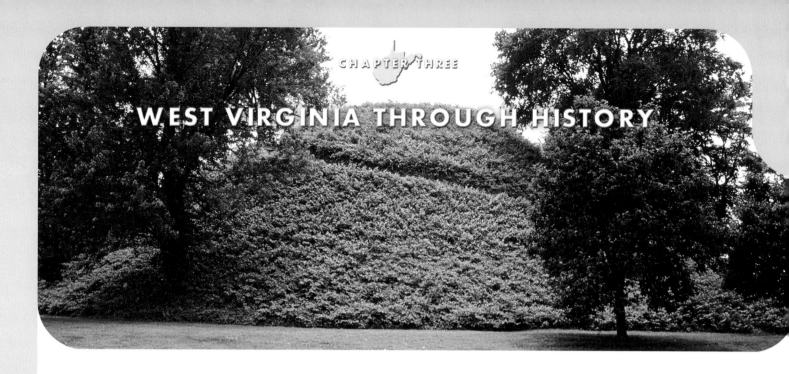

CHAPTER THREE

WEST VIRGINIA THROUGH HISTORY

The first people arrived in present-day West Virginia around 8,000 to 10,000 years ago. They were called Paleo-Indians. They came from present-day Kentucky, Indiana, and Ohio. Paleo-Indians were nomads, which means they traveled to hunt animals for food, and did not build towns or villages.

Paleo-Indians hunted large mammals, such as bison, camels, and woolly mammoths. They also ate berries, nuts, and roots. Scientists have found tools and arrow points left by the Paleo-Indians at campsites along the Ohio River. Scientists do not know what happened to the Paleo-Indians. They may have disappeared because of war, bad weather, loss of food supply, or disease.

By 1000 B.C., new people had moved to present-day West Virginia. These people were the Adena Culture, also known as Mound Builders. They were called Mound Builders because they made piles of earth, or mounds, to use for temples and burials.

The Adena people built Grave Creek Mound over a period of 100 years or more, from 250 to 150 B.C.

Mound Builder cultures lived along the Ohio and Kanawha rivers. These people built a huge mound at what is today called Moundsville. Called Grave Creek Mound, it is the largest conical (cone-shaped) mound in the United States. It is 69 feet (21 m) tall, with a base circumference of 295 feet (90 m). The mound was used for burying people. Along with the skeletons of these ancient people, scientists have also found weapons, jewelry, and glass beads. These items tell us that the Adena people used tools to make jewelry and glass. They also made spearheads for weapons. Like the Paleo-Indians, there are no clear reasons why the Adena disappeared.

Many of West Virginia's earliest settlers lived along the Kanawha River.

By about A.D. 1500, new Native American tribes had moved into the area. Among the groups that lived there were the Lenni-Lenape, the Cherokee, the Conoy, the Susquehannock, the Shawnee, and the Algonquin. These people came to the region to hunt for food. The rugged, tree-covered mountains provided deer, elk, moose, bear, raccoons, and bobcats. Few of these tribes built permanent settlements in today's West Virginia. Instead, they roamed the land and hunted in West Virginia's forests.

By the 1600s, the Iroquois Confederacy controlled most of present-day West Virginia's land along the Ohio River. The Iroquois Confederacy included the Mohawk, Oneida, Onondaga, Cayuga, and Seneca tribes of New York. Although they controlled the area, the Iroquois did not stop other tribes from building villages in West Virginia. The Shawnee settled in an area now called Point Pleasant, and a Lenni-Lenape settlement blossomed at Bulltown.

FIND OUT MORE

Mound Builders lived in many other regions of North America. Three famous mounds are Great Serpent Mound, Monk's Mound, and the Newark Earthworks. Where are they located?

EUROPEANS ARRIVE

In the early 1600s, people from Europe began arriving in North America. The English, in particular, started colonies, or settlements, up and down the Atlantic coast. In 1607, the Jamestown colony, which was controlled by the English government, began along the coast of present-

The mountains blocked settlers from moving to the western part of Virginia.

day Virginia. The colony claimed land as far west as the Mississippi River and as far north as Lake Michigan.

In the beginning, West Virginia was simply the western part of the Virginia colony. Because it was difficult to cross the Allegheny Mountains, few settlers chose to travel beyond the eastern edge of the mountains. However, as the colony became more crowded, Virginia's settlers wanted to find a route through the mountains. The first known European to explore the area was John Lederer in 1669. Lederer explored the western regions of the Virginia colony.

Real exploration of West Virginia began when Robert Fallam and Thomas Batts set out to find a route through the mountains in 1671. Batts and Fallam crossed the Appalachian Mountains and came upon the New River. This finding surprised the men because the New River flowed to the west. However, the pair never traveled beyond the Appalachian Ridge and Valley because the region was too wild and rugged.

It would take more than fifty years before a permanent European settlement was built in the region. The first European settler was Morgan ap Morgan, a Welsh minister from Glamorganshire, Wales. Morgan received a grant for 1,000 acres (405 ha) of land in western Virginia. In 1726, he built a cabin in the area now known as Bunker Hill, on the eastern panhandle. In 1727, Morgan built the first church in present-day West Virginia.

Settlers traveled by riverboat on West Virginia's calmer rivers.

FIND OUT MORE

Many colonial towns were named after places in Europe. Use an atlas to find the countries of these European and Middle-Eastern cities whose names were used in West Virginia: Vienna, Athens, Bethlehem, London, and Plymouth. Then, locate these towns on a map of West Virginia.

Soon, small settlements began along western Virginia's many rivers. The new colonists were Germans, Scots-Irish, and English. Many settlers named towns for cities in their homeland. New Mecklenburg was named for a town in Germany, and Romney after a town in England.

MOVING IN

Following the path of pioneer Daniel Boone, more than 30,000 settlers poured into the area to claim land. They knew that western Virginia had

After a route through the mountains was discovered, settlers poured into western Virginia by the thousands.

plenty of water for drinking, game for food, and trees for building homes. However, the lives of the settlers were demanding. They worked every day from sunup to sundown. Once they laid claim to land, families built log cabins. The logs were cut so they would fit closely together. Gaps between the logs were filled with mud to prevent cold winds from blowing through the cabin.

Pioneers hunted and fished for food, picked nuts and berries, and cleared land for growing crops. Women cooked, washed clothes by hand, wove cloth for sewing, tended crops, and made soap and candles. Children worked alongside their parents from a very early age. It was not uncommon for seven- or eight-year-old girls to bake bread, tend younger children, or cook dinner. Boys helped with plowing, seeding, hunting, and harvests. Parents who knew how to read or do math taught their children in the evening after all chores were done.

Most pioneers felt that land to the west was free for settling, and did not care about native tribes or their rights to live in western Virginia. As more European settlers arrived, the Shawnee, Mingo, and Lenni-Lenape were forced to move farther west. By 1742, most native people living in the area gave up their land to the large number of settlers moving into the region.

The native people had no understanding of owning land. For them, all land belonged to everyone. During the 1700s, Europeans signed treaties, or agreements, with the Iroquois, the Shawnee, and the Lenni-Lenape. The native people did not understand the treaties, and thought that they allowed Europeans to move as far as the Allegheny Mountains.

WHO'S WHO IN WEST VIRGINIA?

Daniel Boone (1734–1820) was a pioneer, woodsman, frontiersman, and scout. He opened the Appalachian Mountains to settlers in the late 1760s. He and his family lived in a cabin along the Kanawha River. Boone represented Kanawha County in the Virginia state legislature.

In fact, the Europeans created treaties that allowed them to take whatever land they wanted.

By the mid-1700s, Native Americans were tired of the land-hungry settlers. They began raiding the new settlements. British troops were sent to the area to build Fort Henry, Fort Lee, and Fort Randolph to provide protection from Native American attacks. These "fort-towns" grew into the cities of Wheeling, Charleston, and Point Pleasant.

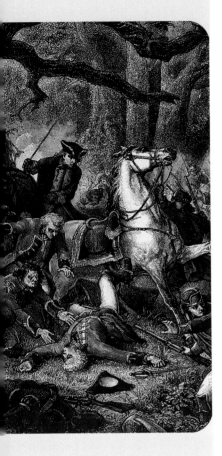

The French and Indian War came about because Great Britain and France both wanted to control fur trading and farmland in the New World.

THE FRENCH AND INDIAN WAR

Just as Europeans and Native Americans struggled over land rights, so did Great Britain and France. In the 1750s, France and England both claimed the Ohio River Valley. Each country wanted to set up trading posts, settlements, and farms, but neither country was willing to let the other have the land. Instead, they fought the French and Indian War (1754–1763) over rights to the Ohio River Valley region. The war got this name because the British found themselves fighting against the French and the Indians.

Many Native Americans sided with the French because they did not try to change tribal ways. The French were more interested in trading with native people. The British, however, took tribal lands as their own. They wanted to change native customs and make native people live as the Europeans did.

Native Americans attacked British forts, creating serious problems for the British. In 1763, Native American warriors led by Ottawa Chief

Pontiac carried out a series of attacks on western Virginia settlements. By mid-summer, Native Americans had captured all the British forts in the region. Ultimately, however, the British army defeated the French and claimed most of the land east of the Mississippi River.

After the war, King George III feared native attacks on settlers moving into western Virginia. He said that no settlers could move west of the Allegheny Mountains. However, Virginians did not listen to the king. Even George Washington headed into western Virginia and claimed large areas of land. In 1768, two treaties forced some of western Virginia's native people to give up their land between the Ohio River and the Allegheny Mountains. The Shawnee, however, did not agree to leave.

In 1773, a businessman named Michael Cresap led a group of settlers to the northwest part of present-day West Virginia. They raided Shawnee towns and murdered native people. Cresap's group killed family members of Mingo chieftain Tah-gah-jute, who was also called James Logan. To get revenge, Tah-gah-jute and his warriors attacked and killed thirteen settlers.

Within a year, the British and the entire Shawnee tribe were at war. The conflict (called Cresap's War or Lord Dunmore's War) ended at the Battle of Point Pleasant in October 1774, where Shawnee Chief Cornstalk led an attack on British troops. The British defeated the Shawnee, forcing them back over the Ohio

England's King George III tried to prevent settlers from moving west of the Allegheny Mountains.

EXTRA! EXTRA!

In 1908, the United States Congress recognized the Battle of Point Pleasant as the first real battle of the American Revolution because it was a fight against British injustice.

River. By 1775, the Lenni-Lenape, the Shawnee, and the Mingo gave up their rights to any land in western Virginia.

THE AMERICAN REVOLUTION

The French and Indian War was expensive for Great Britain, because it was fought thousands of miles from England. Because the British felt that the colonists gained the most benefit, they decided that colonists should pay the costs of the war.

To raise money, the British government passed a number of tax acts or laws against the colonies. These included the Stamp Act, the Townshend Act, and the Quartering Act. These acts required colonists to pay taxes (extra money) on tea, sugar, glass, printed materials, and a long list of other common household items. Colonists resented being taxed without having a say in new laws. They called this "taxation without representation."

In an effort to be heard, people from twelve colonies met at the First Continental Congress in Philadelphia, Pennsylvania. The members wrote to their king to complain about the taxes. The king ignored them.

In 1775, shots were fired between British soldiers and colonial militia at Lexington and Concord, Massachusetts. This was the beginning of the American Revolution (1775–1783), when colonists fought to win freedom from Great Britain. Militia from western Virginia traveled to

Many colonists protested British taxes by rioting in the streets.

Massachusetts to support the colonial war effort. Their trip became legendary, because the men walked 600 miles (966 km) in 24 days. The trip became known as the "Bee Line March" because they traveled as straight and as quickly as possible to reach Massachusetts.

FIND OUT MORE

The militia walked 600 miles (966 km) in 24 days. Roughly, how many miles did they travel each day? Most people walk about 3 miles (4.8 km) per hour. About how many hours per day did the militia walk?

In 1775, representatives from the colonies met in Philadelphia at the Second Continental Congress. Delegates set up an army, led by George Washington, to protect colonists from British troops. The following year, on July 4, 1776, colonial representatives signed the Declaration of Independence. This document said that the colonies no longer belonged to Great Britain, but were free states. However, declaring freedom is different from actually being free. Great Britain was not willing to let go of the colonies so easily, and the war raged on.

In 1782, a group of Native Americans and British troops laid siege to Fort Henry. On September 12, young Betty Zane slipped out of the besieged fort and headed to a cabin about 60 yards (55 m) away. She ran to get a supply of gunpowder for the men in the fort. The natives and the British shot at her, but she was too quick. The extra supply of gunpowder helped the people in the fort to hold off the British, who gave up the siege of Fort Henry and headed to forts that were easier to defeat.

The American Revolution tested the military skills of the Continental Army.

After many years of fighting, the American Revolution ended. The colonies defeated the British Army. As a result, the British government gave up all land between the east coast and the Mississippi River. West Virginia was still considered part of Virginia.

A GROWING NATION

After the war ended, industry slowly came to the western part of the state. Iron smelting and salt mining became major moneymakers. With such an abundance of forestland, timber cutting increased and lumber mills sprouted up. Most of these industries built factories along the area's rivers, as river barges were the only means of transporting finished goods. There were no main roads linking western Virginia to the rest of the state.

Eastern Virginians wanted to take advantage of the natural resources available in the west. However, most rivers in the west flowed westward into the Ohio River. Shipping goods to the east was difficult.

Enterprising easterners decided to build canals that would allow iron and lumber to be brought east to Virginia's major cities, such as Richmond and Norfolk. The Potomac Company would connect the Potomac and Ohio Rivers. The James River Company would build a canal linking the James to the Kanawha.

Despite all this activity to link east and west, the lives of western Virginians were very different from those of eastern Virginians. In the east, the plantation system was the main form of economy. Tobacco plantations thrived on the flat lands of the coastal plain. Plantations are large farms that were worked by slaves. In colonial days, slaves were brought from Africa by ship. They were "owned" by white landowners and were forced to work long hours under poor conditions. Slaves were sold to whomever would pay the most money.

Western Virginians farmed small plots of land, which they worked themselves. Few western Virginians had slaves because they could not afford to buy or keep them. Western Virginia life challenged even the hardiest settlers. Difficult travel, distance, and harsh winter weather isolated the mountain people. The differences between "mountain" life and "flatland" life eventually became a problem for western Virginians.

Meanwhile, the United States faced its own problems in the 1850s and 1860s. The main problem was slavery. The South depended on slaves to keep their plantations running. However, many people, particularly Northerners, disagreed with keeping slaves. One such person was John Brown.

John Brown was an abolitionist who actively fought to free slaves. In 1859, he led a group of men in an attempt to take over the military

WHAT'S IN A NAME?

The names of many places in West Virginia have interesting origins.

Name	Comes From or Means
Spruce Knob	Because the mountain looks like a pine-covered knob
Bluefield	Named for the blue chicory flowers in nearby fields
French Creek	Based on a legend in which three Frenchmen discovered gold there
Hico	Named for a brand of tobacco sold in the area's general store
Moundsville	Named for the large earth mounds built in the area by the Adena
Pocahontas County	Named for a kind Native American woman

John Brown and his men avoided capture for several hours inside the carriage house at Harpers Ferry.

John Brown was a Northerner who strongly opposed slavery.

armory at Harpers Ferry, on the eastern panhandle. The army stored guns, cannons, and bullets at the armory. Brown hoped to lead slaves in a rebellion against their white owners.

Robert E. Lee led United States marines and soldiers against Brown's attack. Brown was arrested and put on trial for treason. At his trial, Brown said, "Had I so interfered in behalf of the rich, the powerful, the intelligent, the so-called great or in behalf of any of their friends. . . every man in this court would have deemed [thought] it an act worthy of reward rather than punishment." Although Brown was not successful (he was convicted and hanged), his actions brought attention to the antislavery issue.

In 1860, Abraham Lincoln was elected the sixteenth United States president. Because Lincoln was against the spread of slavery, the southern states expected the government to pass laws ending slavery. Leaders in the South were worried that their way of life was threatened. They also believed that the United States government did not have the right to tell individual states what to do. Even before Lincoln was sworn in as president, southern states began to secede from, or leave, the United States. They formed their own nation called the Confederate States of America.

There were more than 357,000 people living in western Virginia at the time. Many of these people thought that leaving the Union was a hasty, poorly-made decision. At the Virginia convention in early 1861, thirty-two of the forty-seven delegates from western Virginia voted against leaving the Union. However, the eastern Virginians voted to secede and become part of the Confederate States of America. Western Virginians had no choice but to go along with the more powerful eastern politicians.

Union soldiers set up camp at Harpers Ferry in 1862.

In April 1861, army forces from the Confederate States fired on Fort Sumter in Charleston, South Carolina. This was the first battle of the Civil War (1861–1865). Many western Virginians had ties to both the Union and the Confederacy. In fact, western

Virginia people fought on both sides, and some towns had both Union and Confederate forces drilling on opposite ends of the main street.

There were several Civil War skirmishes on western Virginia soil. The Confederate Army held the town of Grafton and the Monongahela Valley. At the same time, Union forces, led by General McClellan, had orders to control all land north of the Kanawha River. The two forces fought each other at Philippi on June 3, 1861. Historians consider the battle at Philippi to be the first land battle of the Civil War.

Although the Union took over the Monongahela Valley, the Confederacy built a stronghold in the Kanawha Valley. Battles and skirmishes raged along the region's river valleys, as both sides fought for control of western Virginia.

In the eastern part of the state, major battles were fought at Manassas (Bull Run), Fredericksburg, and Chancellorsville. Leading many Confederate troops in these battles was Stonewall Jackson from Clarksburg. Jackson survived three of the worst battles of the Civil War, only to be shot accidentally by one of his own men after winning the battle at Chancellorsville. Upon hearing of Jackson's wound, General Robert E. Lee said, "Could I have directed events, I should have chosen, for the good of the country, to have been disabled in your stead. I congratulate

WHO'S WHO IN WEST VIRGINIA?

Thomas "Stonewall" Jackson (1824–1863) got the nickname "Stonewall" at the battle of Bull Run, when his troops held their line against heavy enemy fire. It was said that he stood like a "stone wall" against the Union.

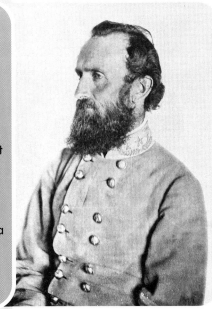

you upon the victory, which is due to your skill and energy." Jackson died a few days later.

Virginia's break from the Union gave western Virginia an opportunity to become a state on its own. In 1861, the western counties held a meeting in Wheeling to discuss separating from Virginia. In the beginning, the western counties formed the Restored State of Virginia. The name then changed to Kanawha.

A year later, in 1862, western Virginians began to set up a government and officially changed their name to West Virginia. President Abraham Lincoln decided that having West Virginia as part of the North would help the Union war effort, and he made West Virginia a state by proclamation on June 20, 1863. As the thirty-fifth state, West Virginia adopted the motto *Montani semper liberi* (Mountaineers are always free). This motto represented the independent nature of people living in the Appalachian Mountains.

The Civil War lasted four long years. In April 1865, Confederate General Robert E. Lee surrendered to Union General Ulysses S. Grant at Appomattox, Virginia. The South had lost in many ways. Slavery came to an end. The South lay in ruins, with roads, railroads, bridges, and cities destroyed in battle.

INDUSTRIAL WEST VIRGINIA

By the end of the 1800s, industry blossomed in West Virginia. (*Industry* means businesses and factories that collect raw materials and make

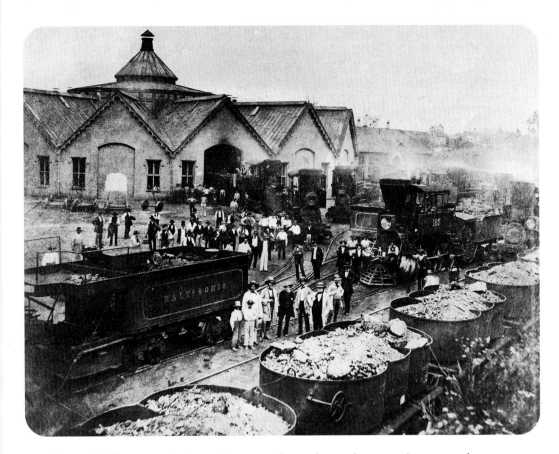

The railroad made it easier to ship coal and timber east for processing.

products.) The new industries were based on the state's natural resources such as coal, natural gas, petroleum, salt, timber, and the mills needed to process these resources. The mines and mills drew European immigrants by the thousands. Transportation became even more important. Several thousand African-Americans moved into West Virginia to build roads and to lay railroad tracks.

Coal was at the heart of the economic boom. Owners opened coal mines along the western edge of the Allegheny Mountains. Mine owners became rich, but the miners themselves did not. Miners dug with company pickaxes, moved coal in company hoppers, and lived by company rules. When they finished work, they shopped in company-owned stores and slept in company-owned houses.

While this might sound ideal, mine owners took advantage of the situation. Owners charged rent on the tools, hoppers, and homes. To make sure that miners spent their money in company-owned stores, many mines paid wages in scrip. Scrip was company-printed "money" that could be spent only in company stores, where prices were high. Often the miners went into debt trying to stay alive.

To make things worse, some miners were cheated out of their fair wages. Because coal miners earned money based on the weight of coal mined, some mine owners cribbed, or cheated, the weights so that miners were not paid for a full load. This is how it was done: The cars used to transport the coal were supposed to hold 2,000 pounds (907 kilograms) of coal. Some cars were built slightly larger, so they could hold 2,500 pounds (1,134 kg). However, the miner was still only paid for 2,000 pounds.

In addition, the mines were terribly unsafe. Many miners were killed in mine cave-ins. Others died in mine fires, or by contracting a disease called "black lung," which resulted from breathing coal dust for years.

In 1890, the West Virginia branch of the United Mine-Workers of America was formed. This labor union fought for safer working conditions, company-paid health care,

The United Mine-Workers of America helped many miners to gain improved working conditions in the mines.

and better pay for the miners. Its members wanted the practice of paying in scrip and running company stores to come to an end. Owners fought against miners joining the labor union. Occasionally, people from both sides were injured in armed fights.

To force mine owners to improve working conditions, miners sometimes refused to work. When miners did not work, the company did not make money. These work stoppages, called strikes, forced mine owners to make safety improvements in the mines. Still, an underground explosion killed 361 people in Monongah in 1907. Despite this horrible accident, mine owners still did not want to make mines safer. They believed that safety cost too much money. Instead, the owners were willing to risk the miners' lives.

Mary "Mother" Jones, an Irish immigrant, spoke out on behalf of West Virginia's miners. Mother Jones was a national labor leader in favor of safer mines, better pay, and healthier working conditions. She once said, "The story of coal is always the same. It is a dark story. For a second's more sunlight, men must fight like tigers. For the privilege of seeing the color of their children's eye by the light of the sun, fathers must fight like beasts in the jungle. That life may have something of decency, something of beauty. . . for this, men who work down in the mines must struggle and lose, struggle and win."

Mother Jones helped call attention to the cause of mine workers.

THE TWENTIETH CENTURY

In the early 1900s, an event took place across the globe that would affect the entire United States, including West Virginia. In 1914, Austria's Archduke Ferdinand was killed while visiting Serbia in Europe. Within days, Germany, Austria-Hungary, and Turkey declared war on Serbia. Serbia had treaties with France and England to help in case of war. Soon, most of Europe was at war. The United States did not immediately enter the war. However, American-made products were sold to the English and French to help the war effort.

As with many other states, World War I (1914–1918) brought prosperity to West Virginia. West Virginia provided steel, iron, and textile products (cloth) for England and France. In 1917, the United States joined the war, after a German submarine sank the USS *Housatonic*, a ship belonging to the United States navy.

Many West Virginians served in the military in Europe. At home, mills, mines, and factories worked to produce steel and iron, coal for fuel, and cloth for bandages and uniforms. This high level of productivity kept West Virginia workers busy and businesses profitable for more than ten years, even after the war ended.

Then, disaster struck. In 1929, the stock market crashed. Banks and businesses across the country lost great amounts of money. People who had saved money in banks or invested in businesses also lost money. The country entered a period of serious economic problems, called the Great Depression (1929–1939).

During the depression, few people could afford to buy new houses, cars, machinery, or even clothing and food. Money problems hit industries hard. With no one to buy company products, factories closed, putting many people out of work. The mines and mills that supplied these factories had no place to sell their raw materials, so they also closed. West Virginia, already poor compared to neighboring states like Virginia, Pennsylvania, and Ohio, became even poorer.

The Great Depression hit West Virginia hard, leaving thousands of miners and farmers out of work.

Thousands of West Virginians lost jobs, homes, and farms. The federal government tried to help by starting programs such as the Civilian Conservation Corps (CCC) and the Works Progress Administration (WPA). These programs provided jobs for out-of-work men and women. Members of the CCC worked in national parks and fought forest fires. The WPA built roads, bridges, schools, and public libraries. The Tygart Dam, completed in 1938, was one project designed to put West Virginians back to work.

It took a war to end the Great Depression. In 1939, Germany invaded Poland. Within days, England and France declared war against Germany. Soon, all of Europe was at war, and once again iron, steel, textiles, and farm products were in demand. World War II (1939–1945) was fought in both Europe and the Pacific. The United States did not immediately enter the war, but it did agree to sell products to England and France. West Virginia factories and mines opened, and workers were once again earning money.

In 1941, Japan attacked the United States Naval Base at Pearl Harbor in Hawaii. The United States immediately declared war on

A mechanic works on an airplane as part of the CCC program in South Charleston.

FAMOUS FIRSTS

- James Rumsey launched the first steamboat in the Potomac River at New Mecklenburg (Shepherdstown) on December 3, 1787.
- The first rural free mail delivery started in Charles Town in October 1896, and then spread throughout the United States.
- The first sales tax became effective July 1, 1921 in West Virginia.
- The world's first electric railroad was constructed between Huntington and Guyandotte.
- West Virginia was the only state to be designated by Presidential Proclamation. President Abraham Lincoln declared statehood on June 20, 1863.

Japan, and joined the war in Europe. Many West Virginian men joined the Armed Forces, leaving manufacturing jobs open. Women, retired workers, and African-Americans filled these jobs. The war ended in 1945 with the surrender of Germany and Japan, but the prosperity that came about because of the war lasted for several years.

SEGREGATION

Unfortunately, not every West Virginian enjoyed the newfound prosperity. Many African-Americans still worked in lower-paid jobs and were denied equal education. Since the Civil War, many southern states passed laws to keep African-Americans and whites separate. These laws were called "Jim Crow" laws, after a cartoon figure from the 1800s. West Virginia's African-American and white children went to separate schools. African-Americans could not use the same drinking fountains, eat in the same restaurants, or use the same restrooms as white people.

Segregation, the practice of separating people because of their race, ended in 1954 when the United States Supreme Court said that "separate but equal education" was neither equal nor legal. This started the

civil rights movement in which African-Americans fought to be treated the same as whites.

West Virginia had to desegregate, or end the racial separation, in their schools. To further the cause of civil rights, the West Virginia Human Rights Commission was created in 1961 to fight racism. Some schools tried to slow desegregation or stop it altogether. In McDowell County, schools began desegregating in 1956. The school board announced that "Schools are no longer to be designated as white or Negro [African-American]. Pupils may enter the schools most convenient to them."

West Virginia has come a long way since the mid-1900s. Mining continues to be important to West Virginia's economy. However, although West Virginians continue to mine coal, problems exist. Safety, pay, working conditions, and health care concerns remain ongoing issues. Many improvements have been made to make mining safer than it was even fifty years ago. New machinery and health programs may further improve working conditions for coal miners.

Miners continue to fight for safer working conditions. These miners are going hundreds of feet below ground level to dig coal.

While the cost of living in West Virginia is lower than most states, so is the income level. The average per person annual pay is $15,714 (2000 statistic) and ranks fiftieth of all states. Few jobs and low pay have created a serious problem for the state.

West Virginia's population is growing very slowly as a result. Many residents leave the state in hope of finding job security in other areas of the country. West Virginia's mines, steel and iron mills, and textile factories cannot compete with the lower prices and cheaper products made in Asia or South America. Many have closed.

The state government is making an effort to bring new business to West Virginia. Computer and electronics industries are moving into the Ohio and Kanawha river valleys. A growing number of federal government facilities offer government service jobs. Tourism, the business of providing food, housing, and entertainment for visitors to the state, has enjoyed tremendous growth in the past ten years. Popular whitewater rafting trips and ski resorts are also helping to turn West Virginia's economy around.

CHAPTER FOUR

GOVERNING WEST VIRGINIA

West Virginia's capitol was completed in 1932 and took eight years to build.

Every state has a constitution that sets down the basic rules and laws that run the government. The West Virginia constitution lists the rights of people living in the state and the powers of its government. The West Virginia government has three branches, or parts: the executive, legislative, and judicial.

The legislative branch makes new laws. The executive branch makes sure state laws are enforced. The judicial branch, made up of courts and judges, interprets the laws. These three branches balance the government so that no one part has too much power.

THE STATE CONSTITUTION

The first West Virginia constitution was adopted in 1863, the year West Virginia became a state. The constitution allowed slavery, but President

Abraham Lincoln insisted that the new state could not be a slave state. A second constitution was written in 1872 and is still used today.

Amendments, or changes, to the constitution are suggested by the legislature or at special meetings called constitutional conventions. When a change is suggested, the state's voters must approve the change before it becomes part of the constitution. At least 51 in every 100 people must vote in favor of the amendment in order for it to pass.

EXECUTIVE BRANCH

The executive branch is responsible for enforcing laws and running state programs. The governor is head of the executive branch. He or she is considered the state's leader and creates programs to improve the quality of life in West Virginia. The attorney general (the state's lawyer), auditor, treasurer, commissioner of agriculture, and secretary of state help the governor to run West Virginia. Voters elect these officers every four years.

The governor is also responsible for signing, or approving, bills (proposed laws). Although a bill may have been passed by the legislature, the governor can reject a bill by using the power of veto. If the legislature thinks the bill is very important, it may override the governor's veto by holding another vote. If 3 in 5 (two-thirds) people in the legislature vote in favor of the bill, it will become a law, even if the governor did not approve it.

The executive branch also includes state departments that are responsible for matters relating to education, agriculture (farming), transportation, and other things. The governor appoints people to run these departments. The executive branch is also responsible for developing a state budget that says how state money will be used.

LEGISLATIVE BRANCH

The legislative branch, sometimes called the legislature, makes state laws. The legislature is made up of two parts: the state senate and the house of delegates. There are thirty-four senators, and each serves a four-year term. There are one hundred delegates who serve two-year terms. West Virginia's lawmakers work in Charleston at the capitol building.

Senators discuss new laws in the senate chamber inside the state capitol.

WEST VIRGINIA GOVERNORS

Name	Term	Name	Term
Arthur I. Boreman	1863–1869	William G. Conley	1929–1933
Daniel D. T. Farnsworth	1869	Herman Guy Kump	1933–1937
William E. Stevenson	1869–1871	Homer A. Holt	1937–1941
John J. Jacob	1871–1877	Matthew Mansfield Neely	1941–1945
Henry M. Mathews	1877–1881	Clarence W. Meadows	1945–1949
Jacob B. Jackson	1881–1885	Okey L. Patteson	1949–1953
Emanuel Willis Wilson	1885–1890	William C. Marland	1953–1957
Aretas Brooks Fleming	1890–1893	Cecil H. Underwood	1957–1961
William A. MacCorkle	1893–1897	William Wallace Barron	1961–1965
George W. Atkinson	1897–1901	Hulett C. Smith	1965–1969
Albert B. White	1901–1905	Arch A. Moore, Jr.	1969–1977
William M. O. Dawson	1905–1909	John D. Rockefeller IV	1977–1985
William E. Glasscock	1909–1913	Arch A. Moore, Jr.	1985–1989
Henry D. Hatfield	1913–1917	Gaston Caperton	1989–1997
John J. Cornwell	1917–1921	Cecil H. Underwood	1997–2001
Ephraim F. Morgan	1921–1925	Robert E. Wise	2001–
Howard M. Gore	1925–1929		

WEST VIRGINIA STATE GOVERNMENT

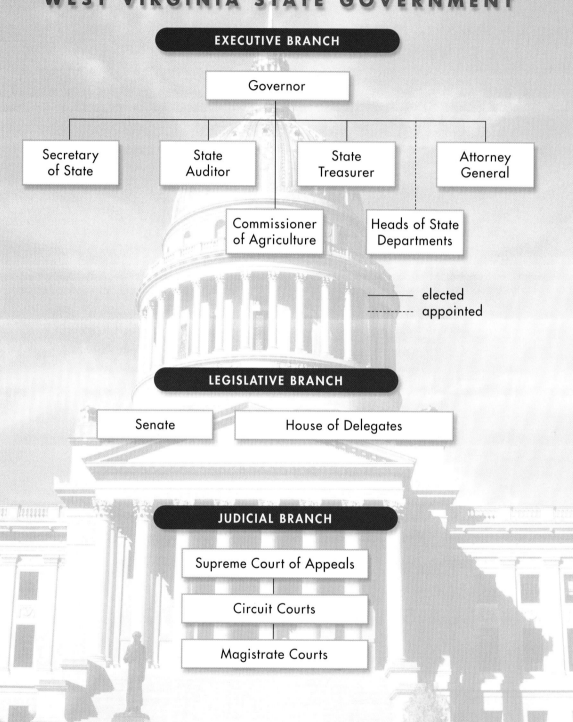

EXECUTIVE BRANCH

Governor

Secretary of State

State Auditor

State Treasurer

Attorney General

Commissioner of Agriculture

Heads of State Departments

——— elected

---------- appointed

LEGISLATIVE BRANCH

Senate

House of Delegates

JUDICIAL BRANCH

Supreme Court of Appeals

Circuit Courts

Magistrate Courts

The legislature meets every year for a sixty-day session. If there are problems that need to be handled at other times, the governor may call a special session of the legislature. For example, an emergency meeting might be held if there is a natural disaster, such as a flood or a severe hurricane.

State laws can cover almost any topic, such as taxes, education, developing land, ecology, or crimes. There are small groups, called committees, within the legislature that focus on various topics concerning the state. These committees review bills to see if they meet the needs of the people. Once a bill passes in committee, it is sent to the senate or house of delegates for a vote. A bill must be approved in both the senate and the house of delegates before it can become a law.

JUDICIAL BRANCH

The judicial branch has several levels of courts. Many cases begin in magistrate courts. Magistrate courts hear cases involving minor crimes, called misdemeanors. For example, if a person is arrested for reckless driving, that person would be tried in magistrate court. The people in charge of these courts, called magistrates, are elected to four-year terms.

Major crimes, called felonies, are heard in circuit court. Examples of major crimes are arson (setting fires), armed robbery, and murder. Circuit court also hears appeals from magistrate court. If a person is not satisfied with the outcome of their trial in magistrate court, they may ask the circuit court to review their case. Sixty-five circuit court judges serve eight-year terms.

The highest or most powerful court in West Virginia is the supreme court of appeals. The supreme court hears appeals from lower courts, and also makes determinations as to the fairness of a law. Five justices (judges) hold office in the supreme court. They serve twelve-year terms.

TAKE A TOUR OF CHARLESTON, THE STATE CAPITAL

Charleston was settled by European colonists in 1794, where the Elk River flows into the Kanawha. In 1885, Charleston was named the capital of West Virginia. The city spreads across both banks of the Kanawha River.

Charleston straddles the Kanawha River.

Charleston was named for Charles Clendenin by his son, the city's founder. Salt mining and lumbering were popular industries when Charleston was founded. The location was ideal for a trading post because it was near Fort Lee. Today, modern office buildings rise up against the clear West Virginia skies.

Charleston is the cultural center of the region. Visitors can listen to country and western fiddlers, bluegrass, jazz, or classical music at the many concerts and festivals held in the city. There are also local and visiting theater groups, ballet troupes, and opera companies.

Our first stop in Charleston is the Capitol Complex. This is where you'll find the governor's office, supreme court of appeals, state senate, and house of delegates. The complex has office buildings, meeting rooms, state records, and the capitol building. The capitol dome glistens bright gold 180 feet (55 m) above the main floor of the building. The capitol itself is furnished with valuable antiques. It features a crystal chandelier that weighs more than 4,000 pounds (1,818 kilograms).

In the Capitol Complex, the West Virginia State Museum

After nightfall, the Capitol Complex is lit with an array of colorful lights.

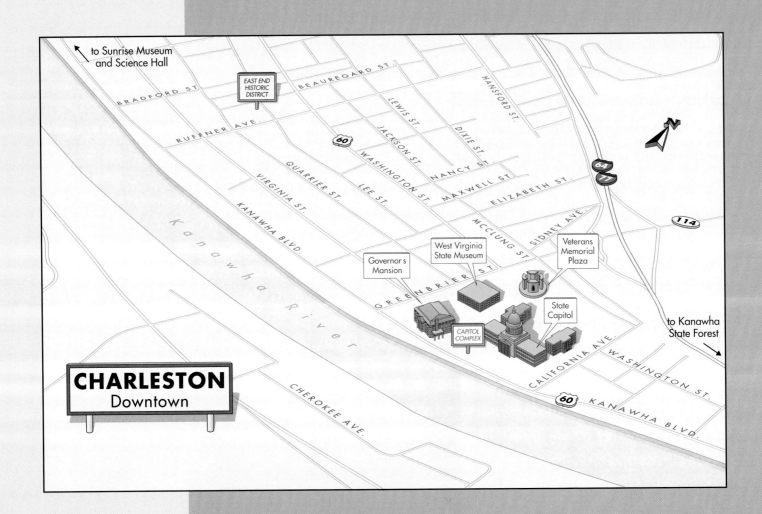

to Sunrise Museum
and Science Hall

EAST END
HISTORIC
DISTRICT

BRADFORD ST.

BEAUREGARD ST.

RUFFNER AVE.

60

QUARRIER ST.

VIRGINIA ST.

KANAWHA BLVD.

LEE ST.

WASHINGTON ST.

JACKSON ST.

LEWIS ST.

NANCY ST.

DIXIE ST.

MAXWELL ST.

HANSFORD ST.

ELIZABETH ST.

McCLUNG ST.

SIDNEY AVE.

GREENBRIER ST.

Kanawha River

Governor's
Mansion

West Virginia
State Museum

Veterans
Memorial
Plaza

CAPITOL
COMPLEX

State
Capitol

CALIFORNIA AVE.

WASHINGTON ST.

KANAWHA BLVD.

60

CHEROKEE AVE.

N

64
77

114

to Kanawha
State Forest

CHARLESTON
Downtown

draws the interest of Civil War buffs. There are many exhibits related to events in the Civil War. Of particular interest is an extensive display about John Brown and the attack on the Harpers Ferry arsenal.

While in the capital, stop by the Sunrise Museum and Science Hall, where the motto is "hands on," not "hands off!" The exhibits cover all areas of science, including electronics, magnetism, plants, and animals. Be sure to catch the planetarium show to learn about constellations, comets, and meteors.

During the year, Charleston hosts a number of fairs and festivals. The Black Cultural Festival is held every February and salutes the African-American contribution to music, art, and entertainment. There is a Creative Arts Festival in April, followed by the Vandalia Gathering, a music festival celebrating the international heritage of West Virginia dance. Each fall, the All West Virginia Boat Racing Championships are held on the Kanawha River. If you'd prefer a slow, relaxing boat trip, try one of the many paddlewheelers that steam along the river each day.

If you enjoy the outdoors, visit the nearby Kanawha State Forest. There are more than 25 miles (40 km) of hiking trails winding through these ancient forests. Cardinals, great horned owls, wrens, and scarlet tanagers nest within the forest. Keep an eye out for raccoons, white-tailed deer, bobcats, and minks as you trek through the park.

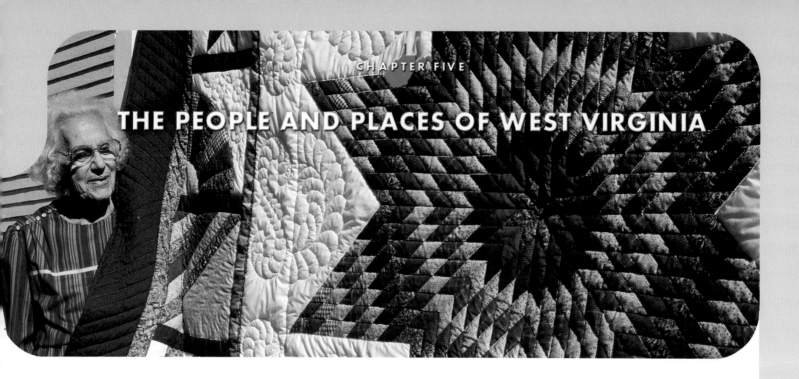

CHAPTER FIVE

THE PEOPLE AND PLACES OF WEST VIRGINIA

Many West Virginians carry on the state's long history of quiltmaking.

According to the **2000 census, 1,808,344 people** live in West Virginia. The state is ranked thirty-seventh in population. Ninety-five in every 100 West Virginians are of European descent. There are very few African-Americans (3 in 100), and fewer than 1 in 100 Hispanic and Asian American people living in West Virginia.

West Virginia's population has decreased since 1980. That year, the state's population was 1,949,664; since then the population has decreased by about 125,000. Of the state's fifty-five counties, only ten show an increase in population over the past ten years. The low population is the result of few jobs and low pay in the state. As jobs are lost, particularly in mining and manufacturing, people leave West Virginia to look for work elsewhere.

FIND OUT MORE

Population distribution tells us where people live. West Virginia's population is 1,808,344. About 4 in every 10 people live in urban, or city, areas. About how many West Virginians live in cities?

WHERE DID THEY COME FROM?

The state's early European settlers were true pioneers, as life in West Virginia was difficult. Among the early settlers were Germans who had originally settled in Pennsylvania when they came to the colonies. An early German settlement was New Mecklenburg, which is today called Shepherdstown. Scots-Irish, Dutch, German, and English people also came to West Virginia before the Civil War.

Most people lived rugged, independent lives. They cleared land for small farms, on which they raised cows for milk, chickens for eggs, sheep for wool, and vegetables for eating. They hunted the woodlands for deer and wild turkey. Women spun thread from wool, then made cloth on simple looms. Many of the handicrafts West Virginia is known for today were part of daily life in colonial days.

Shepherdstown is the oldest permanent European settlement in West Virginia.

GIFTED MOUNTAINEERS

West Virginia has had its share of famous people. Booker T. Washington, born a slave in Malden, grew up to become a famous educator and social reformer. Washington founded the Tuskegee Institute, originally a college for African-Americans, in Alabama. He wrote his life story in a book called *Up from Slavery.*

Booker T. Washington was a major influence on relations between whites and blacks in the South.

Slavery had an impact on many West Virginians. John Brown, a noted abolitionist, fought against slavery by attacking the Harpers Ferry arsenal. Although not as famous, Martin R. Delany was also an abolitionist. He worked with Frederick Douglass to found *The North Star,* an African-American newspaper. Delany became the first African-American major in the United States Army during the Civil War.

Writers from the state have made a mark on American literature. Perhaps the most famous West Virginia writer was Pearl S. Buck, winner of both the Pulitzer Prize and the Nobel Prize in literature. Author Melville Post was known for writing mysteries. Both Mary Lee Settle and Margaret Montague have written about life in West Virginia. Well-known novelist John Knowles wrote *A Separate Peace,* a novel about young men coming of age. Cynthia Rylant, a children's book author who grew up in West Virginia, is a winner of the Caldecott Honor Award for *When I Was Young in the Mountains.*

Athletes have long been heroes for West Virginians. Basketball's Jerry West, born in Cabin Creek, became the first professional basketball player to score more than 4,000 points in a playoff competition. He was an all-American player in high school and college, and is in the Basketball Hall of Fame. In professional baseball, George Brett and Bill Maze-roski were among the most famous players. Brett won the American League batting cham-

pionship twice and was also the 1980 Most Valuable Player in the American League. Mazeroski dominated second base for the Pittsburgh Pirates for seventeen years, but he is best known for hitting a homerun that won the 1960 World Series for Pittsburgh.

In football, West Virginia's Sam Huff played for both the New York Giants and the Washington Redskins. Huff's outstanding performance as a linebacker won him a place in the Football Hall of Fame in 1982. Another football great was Gino Marchetti, also in the Football Hall of Fame.

The darling of West Virginia athletes was tiny spitfire Mary Lou Retton. Retton, born in Fairmont, won the all-around gymnastic gold medal in the 1984 Olympics. Retton is known for scoring a perfect "10" on the vault, a difficult score to achieve.

Mary Lou Retton carried the Olympic Flame during the 2002 Salt Lake Olympic Torch Relay in Houston, Texas.

WORKING IN WEST VIRGINIA

West Virginians work mostly in service positions, such as doctors, nurses, teachers, waiters and waitresses, and hotel managers. These workers provide services rather than products to customers. About 1 in every 4 workers is employed in a service industry. People who work in

Many West Virginians, such as this telephone repairman, work in the service industry.

stores or warehouses account for 2 in every 10 people. Another 2 in 10 people work for state, federal, or local governments. Although mining and farming are important to the state's economy, only 5 in every 100 workers are employed in these fields. Much of the work in mines and on farms is done by machine, so fewer workers are needed in these jobs.

As is true for most states, West Virginia's farms are growing larger in size and fewer in number. In 1955, the state had 69,000 farms. Today, there are fewer than 20,000. The most valuable agricultural products are beef cattle, broiler chickens, turkeys, and dairy products. Grain fields bear hay, oats, and buckwheat. Orchards and vineyards are filled with the sweet aromas of apples, peaches, and grapes.

About $15 of every $100 of state income comes from manufacturing. The most common products include iron and steel, pottery, glass, and textiles. West Virginia has built a solid reputation on the quality and beauty of its art glass. Huntington and Salem produce the most glassware, and many glass factories are open for tours.

West Virginia is known for its fine apples. The Golden Delicious was first grown in the state's orchards many years ago. The recipe below produces a sweet, tasty applesauce that is ideal with pancakes or shortbread cookies.

GOLDEN DELICIOUS APPLESAUCE

3 pounds golden delicious apples
1 cup water
3/4 cup sugar
1 cinnamon stick

Here's what to do:

1. Wash apples. Cut away core and bruised flesh. Cut apples into large chunks, leaving skins intact.
2. Put apples, water, sugar and cinnamon stick in large Dutch oven or heavy saucepan. Put lid on and bring to a boil.
3. As soon as mixture boils, reduce heat to simmer and cook an additional 30–35 minutes, until fruit is very soft.
4. Press fruit and liquid through a strainer into large bowl. Use a wooden spoon to push fruit through strainer.
5. Serve warm with sweet cornbread. Makes 6–8 servings.

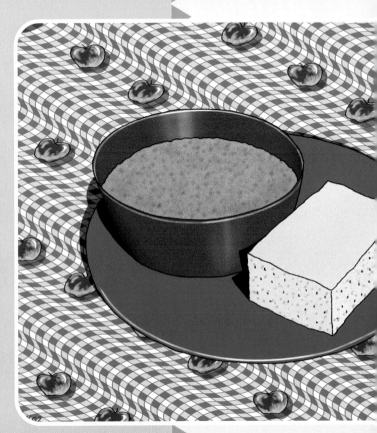

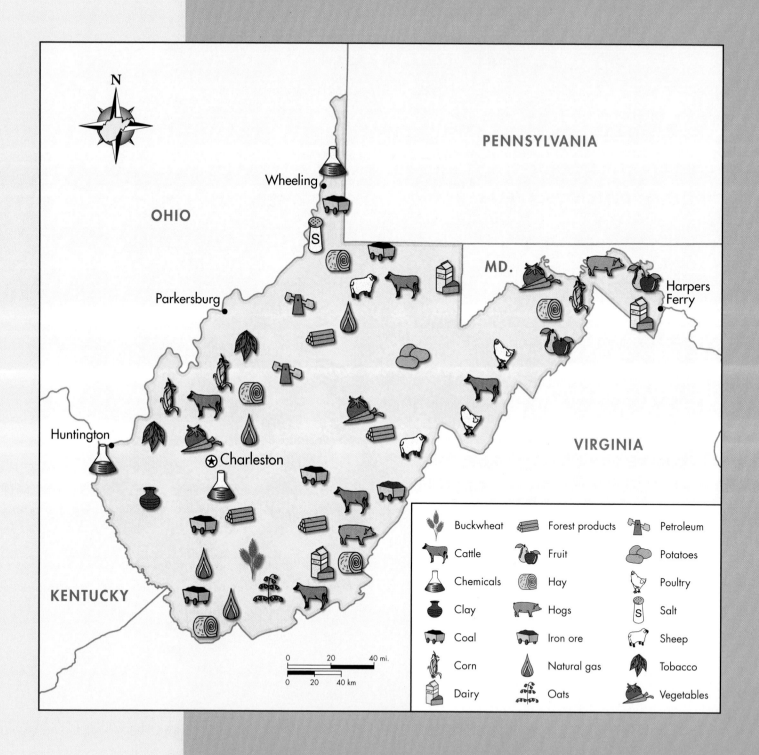

N

PENNSYLVANIA

OHIO

Wheeling

Parkersburg

S

MD.

Harpers
Ferry

Huntington

Charleston

VIRGINIA

KENTUCKY

| 0 | 20 | 40 mi. |
| 0 | 20 | 40 km |

Buckwheat   Forest products   Petroleum

Cattle   Fruit   Potatoes

Chemicals   Hay   Poultry

Clay   Hogs   Salt

Coal   Iron ore   Sheep

Corn   Natural gas   Tobacco

Dairy   Oats   Vegetables

Natural resources add greatly to the state's economy. Lumber products, including hardwoods for furniture, provide work for many people throughout the state. Coal is the most widely mined product, although the state also has natural gas and petroleum. Clay, stone, and gravel are quarried for building materials. In the northeastern part of the state, salt is processed.

A growing industry in West Virginia is tourism. Jobs in the tourist industry include hotel workers, travel guides, restaurant workers, and sports teachers. Each year more than 200,000 people go whitewater rafting on the state's many rivers. The spring brings hikers and fishers. The summer is ideal for kayakers. In fall, tourists come to see the blazing reds, oranges, and golds that paint the landscape. Winter is a skier's haven, with both downhill and cross-country trails.

FIND OUT MORE

What is the difference between natural gas and petroleum? Use an encyclopedia to find the answer.

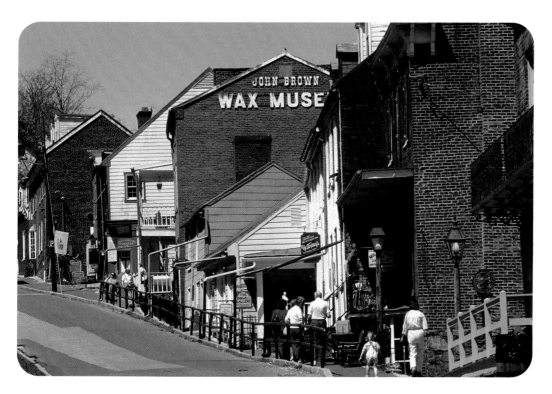

Tourists stroll through the historic district in Harpers Ferry National Historical Park.

Although West Virginia has struggled economically, computer and other electronics companies are bringing more jobs to the state. West Virginia's unemployment rate is higher than the United States average, but is slowly decreasing. Increased tourism will help to overcome the loss of jobs in mines and mills.

TAKE A TOUR OF WEST VIRGINIA

Northern West Virginia

When you plan a trip to West Virginia, be sure to allow time to visit one of the state's many festivals. Northern West Virginia hosts many toe-tapping music events, such as the Wheeling Music Festival. Wheeling also hosts Jamboree U.S.A. at the Capitol Music Hall. You'll hear bluegrass fiddlers, heart-pumping jigs and reels, and plenty of banjo picking. You'll also see clogging, a style of dance that mixes tap dancing and Irish or Scots folk dancing. Clogging got its name from the heavy wooden shoes, called clogs, worn in colonial days.

West Virginians head to Wheeling to show their finest horses at the Oglebay Park Horse Show. The park features a zoo, tennis, fishing, and a museum in an old mansion. The Mansion Museum is

Capitol Music Hall is West Virginia's oldest and largest theater. It was built in 1928 and still features many popular music stars.

known for its beautiful display of art glass. The Good Zoo houses more than eighty-five animal species in their natural settings.

Not far from Wheeling is Moundsville, home of Grave Creek Mound. Built more than two thousand years ago by the Adena culture, this earthwork is the largest cone-shaped mound in the United States.

Along the Ohio River

In downtown Parkersburg, visit the historic Blennerhassett Hotel, built in 1889. The lobby, dining room, and ballroom will give you a sense of Victorian elegance and comfort. Next, stop by the Henry Cooper Log Cabin. This cabin is built from hand-cut logs and was hand-chinked to fill between the holes. You'll get a sense of how pioneers lived, long before the days when wealthy visitors filled the rooms of the Blennerhassett Hotel.

A glassmaker in Huntington skillfully sculpts a fish.

South of Parkersburg in Williamstown, you'll find the Fenton Art Glass Company. The Fenton Art Glass Company makes colored glass that is among the most prized in the country. Books have been written about the beautiful creations by Fenton glass artists. Nearby Huntington is also famous for its handblown art glass. There, the Blenko Glass factory offers demonstrations for visitors. Glassblowing is an unusual art, and watching a blob of molten glass blown

When the Blennerhassett mansion was built in 1798, it was one of the most elegant estates in all of Virginia.

into a delicate piece of art is fascinating. You'll be surprised at the amount of work and skill involved in producing just one stained glass window.

The Huntington Museum of Art offers both an art center and a nature complex. Of course, Appalachian Mountain arts, such as wood carving, quilting, and needlework, are on display. Among the many intricately sewn quilts are wedding ring, log cabin, and bear claw patterns. The museum also features exhibits of fine silverware and handblown glass. Outside the complex are nature trails and an observatory where visitors can gaze at the stars through a high-powered telescope.

As long as you are in the area, visit Blennerhassett Island. There, Aaron Burr and Harmann Blennerhassett plotted to overthrow the government and form a new one of their own. Burr, Blennerhassett, and their colleagues were arrested for treason. Although Blennerhassett was never brought to trial, he soon lost all his possessions, including a mansion on Blennerhassett Island. The mansion and grounds now make up a historic park. Getting to Blennerhassett Island is half the fun—you'll travel on an old-fashioned sternwheeler across the Ohio River.

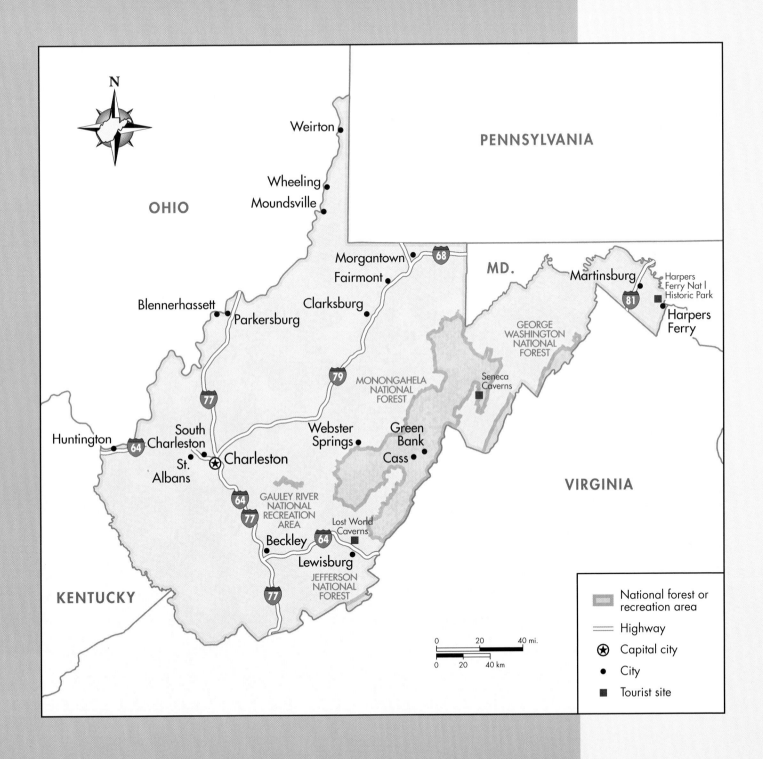

N

PENNSYLVANIA

OHIO

Weirton

Wheeling
Moundsville

Morgantown **68**
Fairmont   MD.

Blennerhassett   Clarksburg   Martinsburg   Harpers
Parkersburg   Ferry Nat'l
                                                         Historic Park
                          GEORGE
                          WASHINGTON   **81**
                          NATIONAL
                          FOREST   Harpers
                                                Ferry

                    79
                          MONONGAHELA
                          NATIONAL   Seneca
                          FOREST   Caverns
            77

Huntington   Webster   Green
        South   Springs   Bank
        Charleston   Cass   VIRGINIA
        St.   **64** Charleston
        Albans
                                GAULEY RIVER
                    64   NATIONAL
                                RECREATION
                    77   AREA
                          Lost World
                          Caverns
                    Beckley **64**
KENTUCKY   Lewisburg
                    77 JEFFERSON
                          NATIONAL
                          FOREST

0   20   40 mi.

0   20   40 km

National forest or
recreation area

Highway

Capital city

City

Tourist site

65

Southern West Virginia

Tiny Lewisburg is an important stop on any West Virginia tour. The Old Stone Church is the oldest church west of the Allegheny Mountains. Services are still held in the church, which features hand-carved woodwork.

Nearby, the Lost World Caverns contain several rooms filled with strange rock formations. Cave hunters from Virginia discovered the caverns in 1942. Since then, the caves have become a popular tourist attraction.

During World War II, Japanese Americans lived in a detention center near White Sulphur Springs, called the Greenbrier. The main building served as a hospital during the Civil War. Visitors should also check out the bunker in which the U.S. president and members of Congress were to be taken in case of a nuclear attack on the United States.

Eastern West Virginia

A woodchopping festival in Webster Springs lets lumberjacks show off their talents at felling trees, stripping bark, and logrolling. Winter Ski Carnival challenges downhill racers and slalom experts. Arts and crafts enthusiasts enjoy quilting, making pottery, and woodworking festivals.

One sport that draws plenty of tourists is *spelunking*, the official word for exploring caves. West Virginia is dotted with caves, both large and small. Seneca Cavern is the largest cave system in the state. These caverns have underground lakes, spectacular rock formations, and an

eerie sense of wonder. Seneca Rocks attracts rock climbers who like to test their skills on the 900-foot (274-m) stone cliffs.

In Green Bank, be sure to visit the National Radio Astronomy Observatory. This site records and studies radio waves from space. The visitor's center offers a chance to see the telescopes and view a film about radio telescopes and what they do.

If you'd like a relaxing, breathtaking trip, try the state-run scenic railroad that leaves from a station in Cass. The train passes through

Autumn leaves cover the ground in a carpet of yellow.

some of the most beautiful mountain country in the United States. Fall trips are especially beautiful, as the woodland is afire with brightly colored leaves.

For history buffs, there is the Harpers Ferry National Historical Park where abolitionist John Brown took over the army weapons arsenal. Brown was tried and hanged for treason in Charles Town, where a stone marker notes the event.

There are festivals held for many of the crops produced in the state, including buckwheat, apples, tomatoes, tobacco, black walnuts, and strawberries.

West Virginia has something for everyone. Delicate glassworks and fine old buildings blend in with the rugged, mountainous landscape. West Virginia's history rests in the earthworks of the Adenas and the battlefields of the Civil War. The state's future lies in its natural beauty. People flock to West Virginia for the stunning scenery and adventurous outdoor life that mountaineers have enjoyed for years.

Glade Creek Grist Mill captures the scenic beauty and unique history that is West Virginia.

WEST VIRGINIA ALMANAC

Statehood date and number: June 20, 1863; 35th state

State seal: The seal contains the state motto. A stone in the center of the seal stands for strength. On the stone is the date West Virginia was admitted to the Union, June 20, 1863. The farmer represents agriculture. The miner represents industry. Adopted in 1863.

State flag: A white background with a dark blue border around the edges. In the center is the state seal, surrounded by clusters of rhododendron, the state flower. Adopted in 1929.

Geographic center: Braxton, 4 miles (6.4 km) southeast of Marshfield

Total area/rank: 24,231 square miles (62,758 sq km)/41st

Borders: Ohio, Kentucky, Pennsylvania, Virginia, and Maryland

Latitude and longitude: West Virginia is located at approximately 37° 16' N to 40° 37' N by 77° 45' W to 82° 19' W.

Highest/lowest elevation: Spruce Knob, 4,861 feet (1,482 m)/ Potomac River, Jefferson County, 240 feet (73 m) above sea level

Hottest/coldest temperature: 112° F (44° C) on July 10, 1936, at Martinsburg/–37° F (–38° C) on December 30, 1917, at Lewisburg

Land area/rank: 24,119 square miles (62,468 km)/41st

Inland water area: 112 square miles (290 sq km)

Population (2000 Census)/rank: 1,808,344/37th

Population of major cities:

   Charleston: 53,421

   Huntington: 51,475

   Parkersburg: 33,099

   Wheeling: 31,419

Origin of state name: Named for England's Queen Elizabeth I, the Virgin Queen

State capital: Charleston

Counties: 55

State government: 34 senators, 100 delegates

Major rivers/lakes: Ohio, Kanawha, New, Big Sandy, Monongahela, Little Kanawha, and Potomac/Summersville, Sutton, Bluestone, Tygart, East Lynn

Farm products: Apples, peaches, hay, tobacco, corn, wheat, oats

Livestock: Chickens, cattle, hogs

Manufactured products: Machinery, plastic and hardwood products, glass, metals, chemicals, aluminum, steel

Mining products: Coal, natural gas, clay, dolomite, sandstone, shale, salt, gravel

Fishing products: Bass, pike, bluefish, carp, catfish, walleye, trout, muskie

Animal: Black bear

Bird: Cardinal

Butterfly: Monarch

Color: Old-gold and blue

Fish: Brook trout

Flower: Rhododendron

Fruit: Golden delicious apple

Grass: Bluegrass

Mineral: Coal

Motto: *Montani semper liberi:* "Mountaineers are always free"

Nickname: The Mountain State

Rock: Limestone

Song: "The West Virginia Hills," words by Ellen King and music by H. E. Engle

Tree: Sugar maple

Wildlife: Black bears, white-tailed deer, skunks, beavers, gray and red foxes, minks, opossums, groundhogs, rabbits, frogs, toads, snakes, turtles, hawks, eagles, wild turkeys, grouses, bobwhites, cardinals, scarlet tanagers, blackbirds, crows, wrens, sparrows

TIMELINE

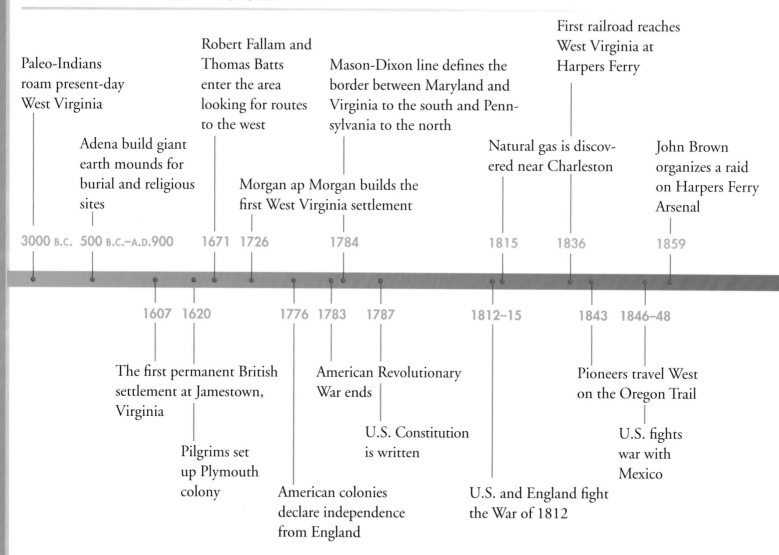

Paleo-Indians roam present-day West Virginia

Adena build giant earth mounds for burial and religious sites

Robert Fallam and Thomas Batts enter the area looking for routes to the west

Morgan ap Morgan builds the first West Virginia settlement

Mason-Dixon line defines the border between Maryland and Virginia to the south and Penn-sylvania to the north

Natural gas is discovered near Charleston

First railroad reaches West Virginia at Harpers Ferry

John Brown organizes a raid on Harpers Ferry Arsenal

3000 B.C.   500 B.C.–A.D. 900   1671   1726   1784   1815   1836   1859

1607   1620   1776   1783   1787   1812–15   1843   1846–48

The first permanent British settlement at Jamestown, Virginia

Pilgrims set up Plymouth colony

American colonies declare independence from England

American Revolutionary War ends

U.S. Constitution is written

U.S. and England fight the War of 1812

Pioneers travel West on the Oregon Trail

U.S. fights war with Mexico

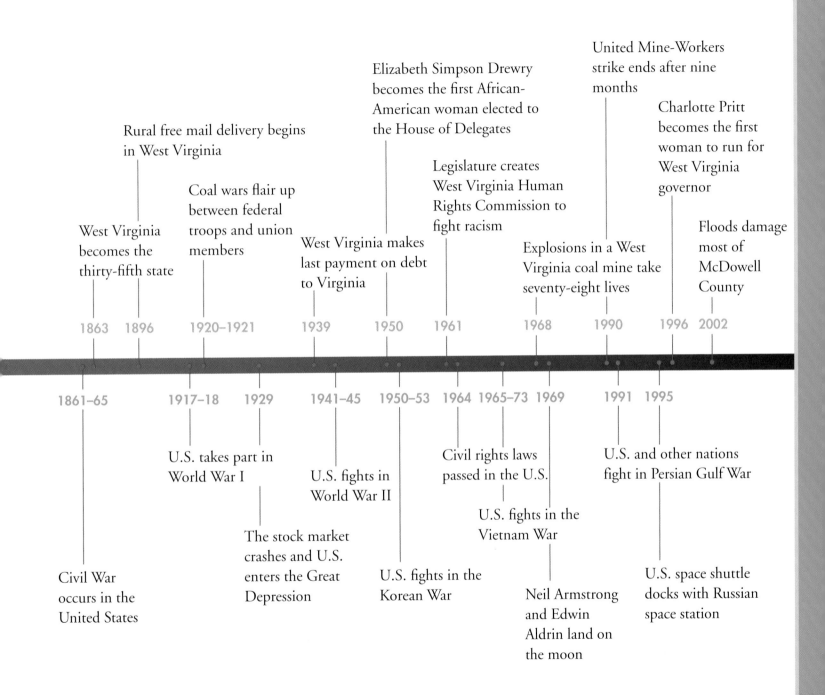

United Mine-Workers strike ends after nine months

Elizabeth Simpson Drewry becomes the first African-American woman elected to the House of Delegates

Rural free mail delivery begins in West Virginia

Charlotte Pritt becomes the first woman to run for West Virginia governor

Legislature creates West Virginia Human Rights Commission to fight racism

Coal wars flair up between federal troops and union members

Floods damage most of McDowell County

West Virginia becomes the thirty-fifth state

West Virginia makes last payment on debt to Virginia

Explosions in a West Virginia coal mine take seventy-eight lives

1863   1896   1920–1921   1939   1950   1961   1968   1990   1996   2002

1861–65   1917–18   1929   1941–45   1950–53   1964   1965–73   1969   1991   1995

U.S. takes part in World War I

Civil rights laws passed in the U.S.

U.S. and other nations fight in Persian Gulf War

U.S. fights in World War II

U.S. fights in the Vietnam War

The stock market crashes and U.S. enters the Great Depression

U.S. fights in the Korean War

U.S. space shuttle docks with Russian space station

Civil War occurs in the United States

Neil Armstrong and Edwin Aldrin land on the moon

GALLERY OF FAMOUS WEST VIRGINIANS

Belle Boyd
(1843–1900)
Writer, actress, and accomplished spy for the Confederacy during the Civil War. Born in Martinsburg.

Martin R. Delany
(1812–1885)
First African-American major in the United States Army. Founder of *The North Star* newspaper (with Frederick Douglass), which promoted ending slavery. Born in Charleston.

Anna Jarvis
(1864–1948)
Started a campaign to celebrate Mother's Day. Born in Webster.

John S. Knight
(1894–1981)
Publisher and founder of the Knight-Ridder chain of newspapers. Knight-Ridder publishes newspapers in thirty-two U.S. cities, including Charlotte, North Carolina; Detroit, Michigan; and Fort Worth, Texas. Born in Bluefield.

John Knowles
(1924–2001)
Author of *A Separate Peace, Spreading Fires, Phineas,* and *The Paragon. A Separate Peace*, written in the 1950s, is still assigned reading in many middle and junior high schools. Born in Fairmont.

Mary Lou Retton
(1968–)
1984 Olympic Gold Medal winner in gymnastics. Born in Fairmont.

Walter P. Reuther
(1907–1970)
Labor leader and former president of United Auto Workers (AFL-CIO). Born in Wheeling.

Booker T. Washington
(1856–1915)
Black educator, leader, and founder of Tuskegee Institute, a college for African-Americans. Lived in Malden.

Jerry West
(1938–)
Former professional basketball star of the Los Angeles Lakers. Born in Cabin Creek.

Brigadier General Charles Yeager, U.S.A.F. Retired
(1923–)
First person to fly faster than the speed of sound, on October 14, 1947. Born in Myra.

GLOSSARY

agriculture: the study and practice of farming

amendment: a change in a law or document

capital: the city that is the center of a state or country government

capitol: the building in which a government meets

circumference: the distance around the outside of a circle

climate: an area's weather conditions over a long period of time

constitution: basic rules and laws that run a government

depression: a period during which money is scarce and businesses close

economy: how a country makes money

felony: a serious crime, such as robbery or murder

gorge: a long, narrow, and deep hollow between hills

interpret: to explain the meaning of something

manufacturing: making products, such as cars or lamps

militia: an untrained, nonprofessional army

misdemeanor: a minor crime, such as illegal parking or speeding

plantation: a large farm that grows one main cash crop

population: the number and mix of people in a region

proclamation: an official announcement

prosperity: financial well being

racism: disliking a person or treating a person badly because of the color of his or her skin

reservoir: a man-made lake, built to hold water

rural: in open country or farmland

textile: having to do with making thread, yarn, or cloth

tourism: the business of providing shelter, food, and entertainment for visitors

transportation: a system of roads, trains, buses, and airports

treason: the act of working against the better interests of a country

unemployment: the condition of being without a job

union: a group of workers who join together to get better pay or working conditions

FOR MORE INFORMATION

Web sites

The State of West Virginia
http://www.state.wv.us/
Information about West Virginia government, news, and communities.

West Virginia Tourism
http://www.callwva.com/
Things to do and see in the state, including events, photos, and attractions.

West Virginia State and Local Government
http://lcweb.loc.gov/global/state/wv-gov.html
All about the state, county, and city governments of West Virginia.

West Virginia Sites
http://www.westvirginia.com/
A variety of links to West Virginia sites.

Books

Anderson, Joan Wilkins and George Ancona. *Pioneer Children of Appalachia*. New York, NY: Clarion Books, 1990.

January, Brendan. *John Brown's Raid on Harpers Ferry*. Danbury, CT: Children's Press, 2000.

Lawlor, Laurie. *Daniel Boone*. Morton Grove, IL: Albert Whitman & Co., 1991.

Marsh, Carole. *Jurassic Ark! West Virginia Dinosaurs and Other Prehistoric Creatures*. Peachtree City, GA: Gallopade International, 1994.

Addresses

Office of the Governor, West Virginia
State Capitol
Charleston, WV 25305

West Virginia Department of Tourism
Department of Commerce
West Virginia Division of Tourism
State Capitol
Charleston, WV 25305

West Virginia National Forest Information
U.S. Forest Service
200 Sycamore Street
Elkins, WV 26241

Charleston Convention and Visitors Bureau
200 Civic Center Drive
Charleston, WV 25301

INDEX

ABOUT THE AUTHOR

Barbara A. Somervill enjoys writing for children. She says, "The challenge is to find interesting information and present it in a way that children can understand and enjoy." To find information about West Virginia, she checked out a number of sources such as the Internet, Chambers of Commerce and tourist bureaus, and the local library.

Barbara was raised and educated in New York State. She also lived in Toronto, Canada; Canberra, Australia; Palo Alto, California; and Simpsonville, South Carolina. She is the mother of four boys, two dogs, and a cat; and the proud grandmother of Lilly.